AF413520

WHAT DOES THE US ARMY DO?

GOVERNMENT BOOKS 7TH GRADE CHILDREN'S GOVERNMENT BOOKS

The United States Military is comprised of one of the world's largest and most powerful armies. For fiscal year 2017, the projected number of personnel, including active duty end strength personnel, is 1,281,900, with an additional 801,200 people serving in the seven additional reserve components. Read further to learn about the U.S. Military and its branches.

THE U.S. ARMED FORCES

The United States Armed Forces consist of five armed branches: Air Force, the Coast Guard, the Navy, Marine Corps, and the Army. Generally, there are three distinct categories of military people: active duty, reserve and guard forces, and retirees and veterans.

Battle of Long Island

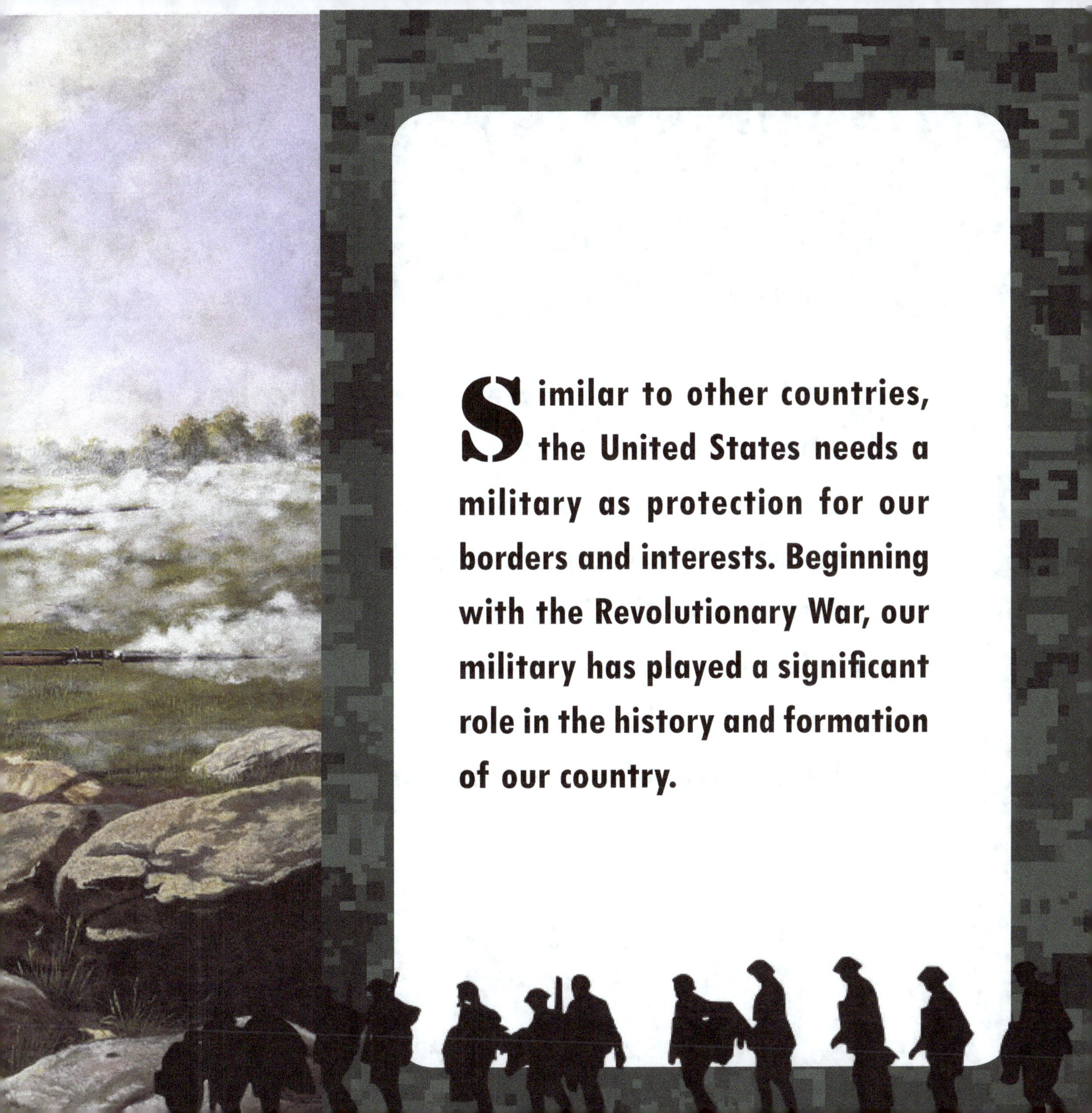

Similar to other countries, the United States needs a military as protection for our borders and interests. Beginning with the Revolutionary War, our military has played a significant role in the history and formation of our country.

WHO'S IN CHARGE?

As Commander in Chief, the President of the United States is responsible for final decisions. The Secretary of the Department of Defense maintains control over the military and each of its branches, with the exception of the Coast Guard, which is under the control of Department of Homeland Security. Having more than 2 million military and civilian employees, the Department of Defense is the largest employer in the world.

Attack on Pearl Harbor

WOMEN IN THE MILITARY

In 1942, the Woman's Army Auxiliary Corps was established in the U.S. On December 7, 1941, during the Pearl Harbor attacks, women saw combat during World War II as nurses.

Demobilization after WWII let to a great majority of women that were serving in the Armed Forces being returned to life as a civilian. Signed by President Truman, the Women's Armed Services Act of 1948 allowed women to serve during times of peace

in fully integrated units, and the WAC remained as a separate female unit. Many women served in the Mobile Army Surgical Hospitals during the Korean War of 1950-1953.

The first six female aviators obtained their wings in 1974, as naval pilots. The prohibition of women in combat, mandated by Congress, placed limitations on their advancement, however, at least two of them retired as captains. The Gulf War in 1991 proved to be a critical time for women's roles in the Armed Forced to be brought to the media's attention around the world. There are several reports of women engaging with enemy forces during this conflict.

Female US Military Soldier

Navy SEALs

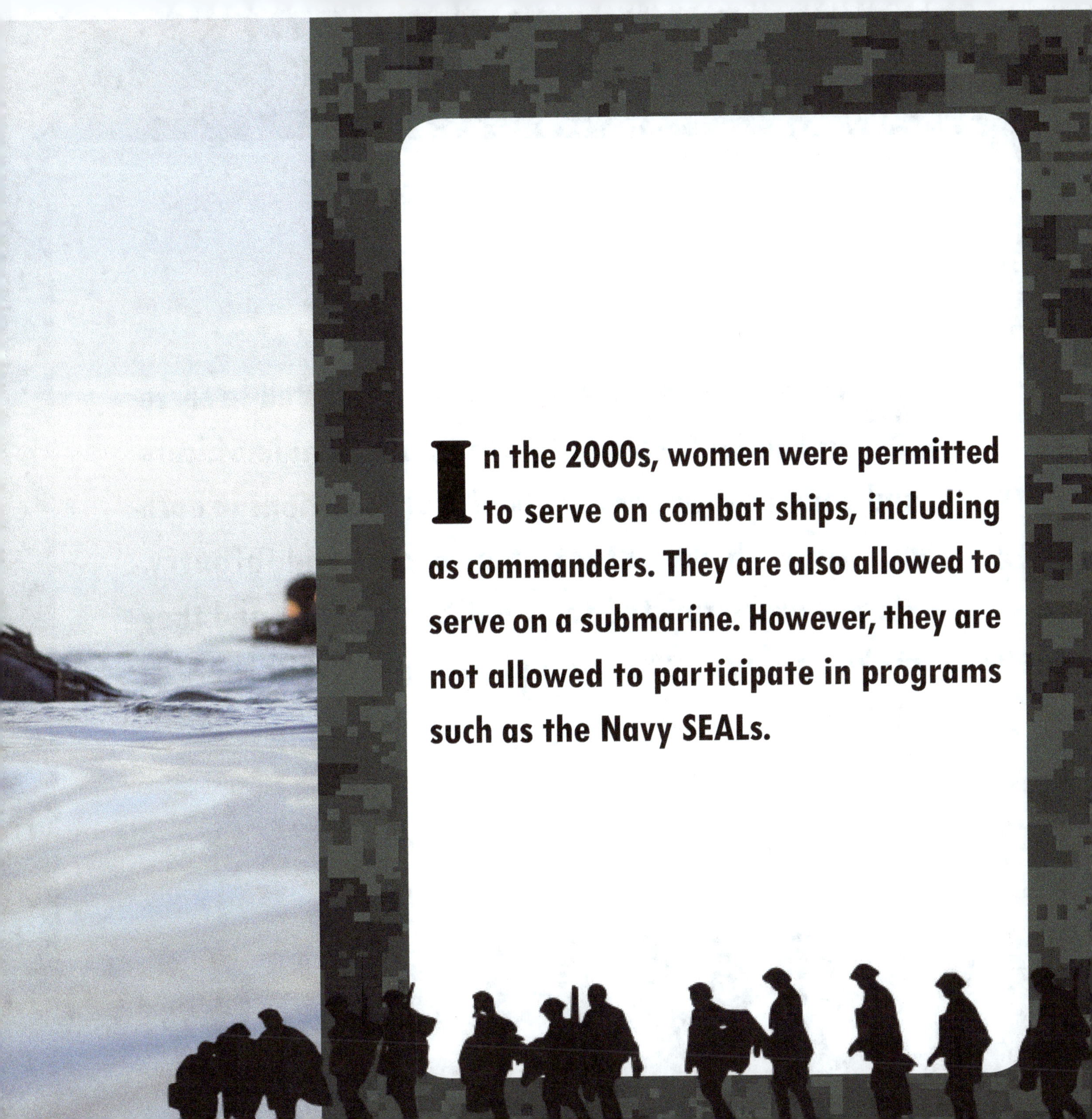

In the 2000s, women were permitted to serve on combat ships, including as commanders. They are also allowed to serve on a submarine. However, they are not allowed to participate in programs such as the Navy SEALs.

Female enlisted soldiers are not permitted to serve in Special Forces or Infantry, but female officers and enlisted members can hold staff positions in each branch, with the exception of armor and infantry. Women are permitted to fly military aircraft and they make up about 2% of all pilots enlisted in the U.S. Military.

On December 3, 2015, Ashton Carter, the United States of America Secretary of Defense, announced that all combat jobs would be available to females. This provided women

with access to approximately 10% of military positions which previously were not available to them because of their combat nature.

This decision provided the military until January 2016 to obtain exceptions if they felt that certain jobs should be restricted to men. These restrictions came about due to previous studies that stated that units of mixed genders would be less capable when in combat. The physical requirements for all positions remained unchanged.

American Civil War

THE DRAFT

Commonly referred to as the draft, Conscription in the United States, has been utilized by the United States federal government during these four conflicts: the American Civil War, World War I, World War II, and the Korean and Vietnam Wars (known as the Cold War).

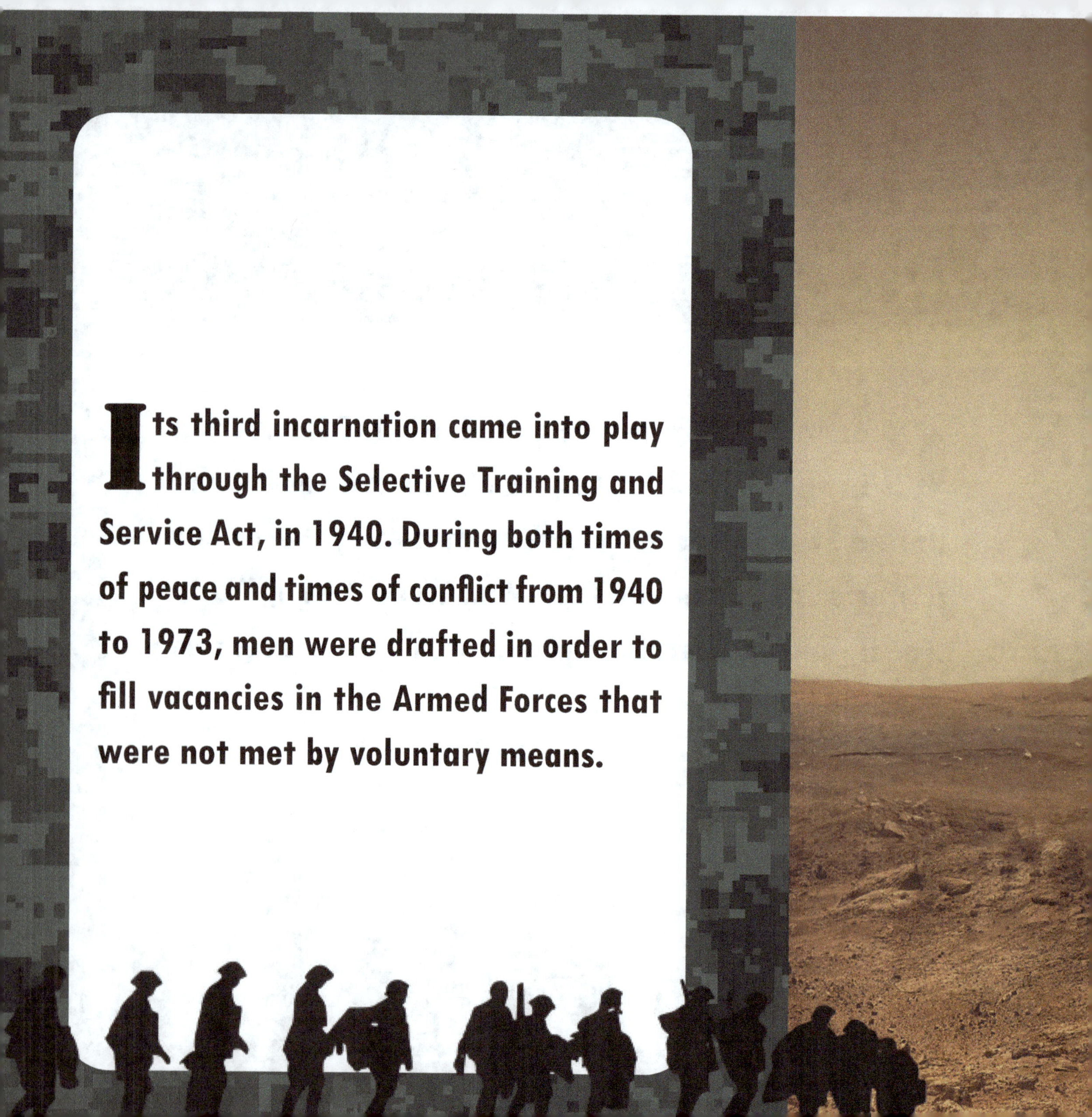

Its third incarnation came into play through the Selective Training and Service Act, in 1940. During both times of peace and times of conflict from 1940 to 1973, men were drafted in order to fill vacancies in the Armed Forces that were not met by voluntary means.

U.S. Armed Forces

The draft came to conclusion once the U.S. Armed Forces began a military force of all volunteers. However, as a contingency plan, the Selective Service Systems remains intact, stating that all male civilians that are between the age of 18 and 25 must register so a draft can be resumed quickly if the need arises.

WHAT ARE THE REQUIREMENTS TO JOIN?

In order to join the enlisted ranks, you must typically be a citizen of the United States or a Green Card holder and must be able to read, write, and speak English fluently and must currently reside in the United States.

Military Recruitment Event

You must be in good health, be between the ages of 17 and 40 (depending on the branch of service), hold a high school diploma (some branches accept a GED), and you have to be able to pass the ASVAB (Armed Services Vocational Battery) test. If you have attended college you can join as an officer.

ARMY

The Army is the military's largest branch and the main ground force. Its job is to fight and control using artillery, tanks and land troops.

The Army is a uniformed military service that is part of the Department of the Army, which is one part of three military departments of Department of Defense.

It is led by a senior appointed civil servant (civilian), known as the Secretary of the Army, as well as the Chief of Staff of the Army.

It participates in worldwide conflicts and is the major defensive force and ground-based offensive of the United States.

Fighter Jet

AIR FORCE

The Air Force is the branch of our military that fights with aircraft, which includes bombers and fighter planes. It was considered part of the Army until 1947 when it was developed into a branch of its own. The Air Force is responsible for the military satellites.

This branch is organized under the Department of the Air Force, and is one of three military departments under the Department of Defense. The Secretary of the Air Force is a civilian that is appointed by the President with confirmation by the Senate and reports to the Secretary of Defense. The Chief of Staff of the Air Force is the highest-ranking officer and supervises the Air Force units, as well as serving on the Joint Chiefs of Staff.

Fighter Planes

U.S. Navy Warship

NAVY

This branch fights in seas and oceans worldwide. It uses all types of battleships that includes submarines, aircraft carriers and destroyers. It is quite bigger in size than any other navy throughout the world and, as of 2014, is equipped with 10 out of 20 aircraft carriers worldwide.

It is managed administratively by the Department of the Navy, which is led by the Secretary of the Navy, a civilian. The Department of the Navy itself is a division of Department of Defense, headed by the Secretary of Defense. The Chief of Naval Operations is a four-star admiral and the Department of the Navy's senior naval officer.

US Navy Destroyer

MARINE CORPS

The Marines are the chief landing force of the military. They work closely with the Navy in attacking and establishing the "beachheads" during war. They are typically some of the first soldiers entering combat.

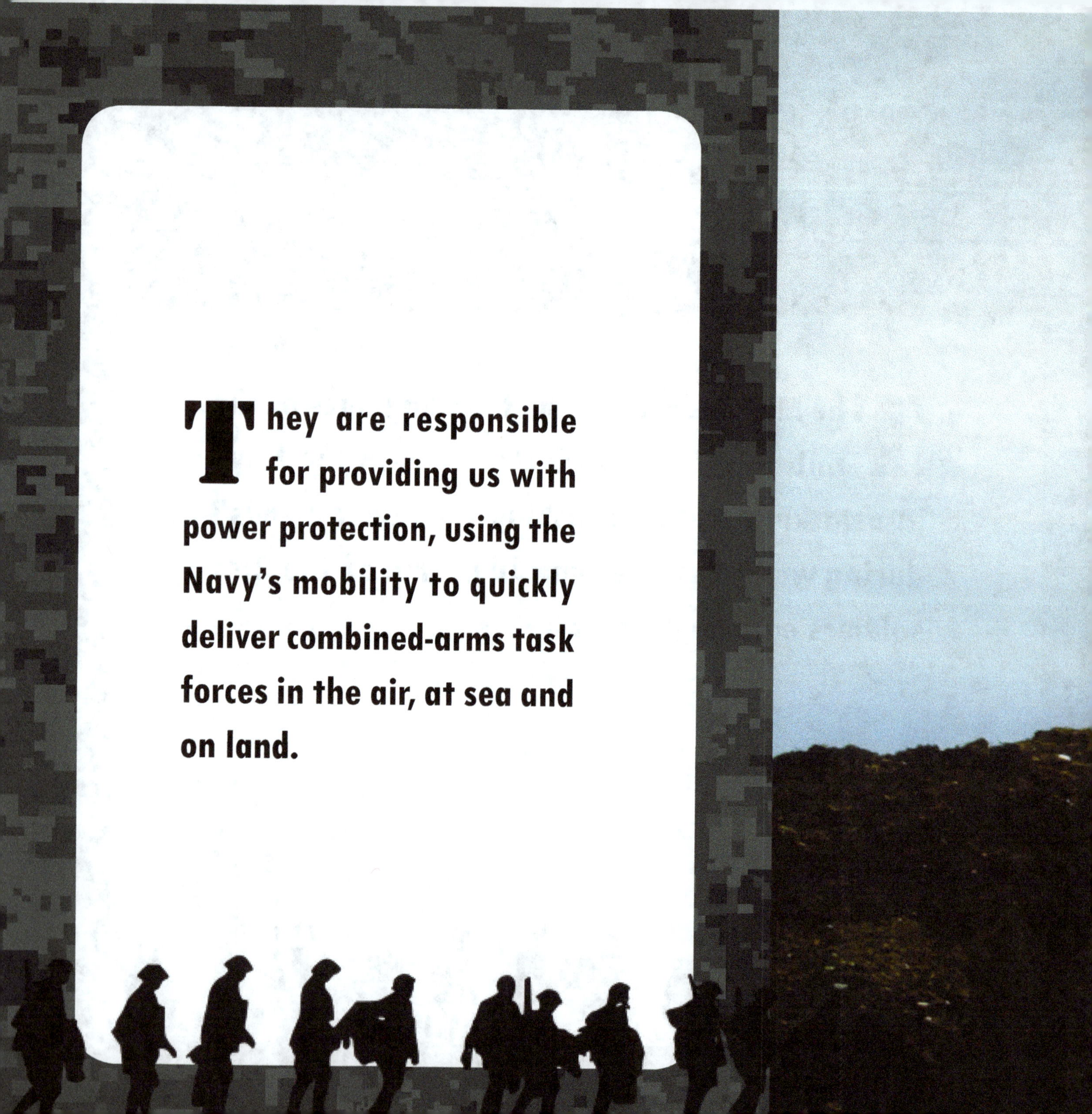
They are responsible for providing us with power protection, using the Navy's mobility to quickly deliver combined-arms task forces in the air, at sea and on land.

The Marine Corps is one of four branches of armed services in the Department of Defense. It is also one of seven uniformed services of the U.S.

By the middle of the 20th century, the Marine Corps became the world's foremost expert of amphibious warfare. Their ability to respond rapidly on a short notice to expeditionary crises gave it a strong role in execution and implementation of American foreign policy.

Combat Scene

Coast Guard Boat

COAST GUARD

The Coast Guard is part of the Department of Homeland Security, which separates it from the other military branches. It is the smallest branch of military. Its duties include monitoring the coastline of the United States, enforcing the border laws, and assists with rescues in the ocean. During times of war, the Coast Guard can become a part of the Navy.

The modern Coast Guard was created by a merging of the U.S. Life-Saving Service and the Revenue Cutter Service under the Department of the Treasury on January 28, 1915. Since it is one of our country's

branches of armed services, it has been a part of each United States war from 1790 through the Iraq War, as well as the War in Afghanistan.

RESERVES

Each branch discussed above consist of active and reserve personnel. While active personnel work full time, the reserves more than likely work at non-military jobs, and train on certain weekends throughout the year. The reserves can be called upon to work full time for the military during times of war.

The U.S. Armed Forces are all essential in protecting our great country.

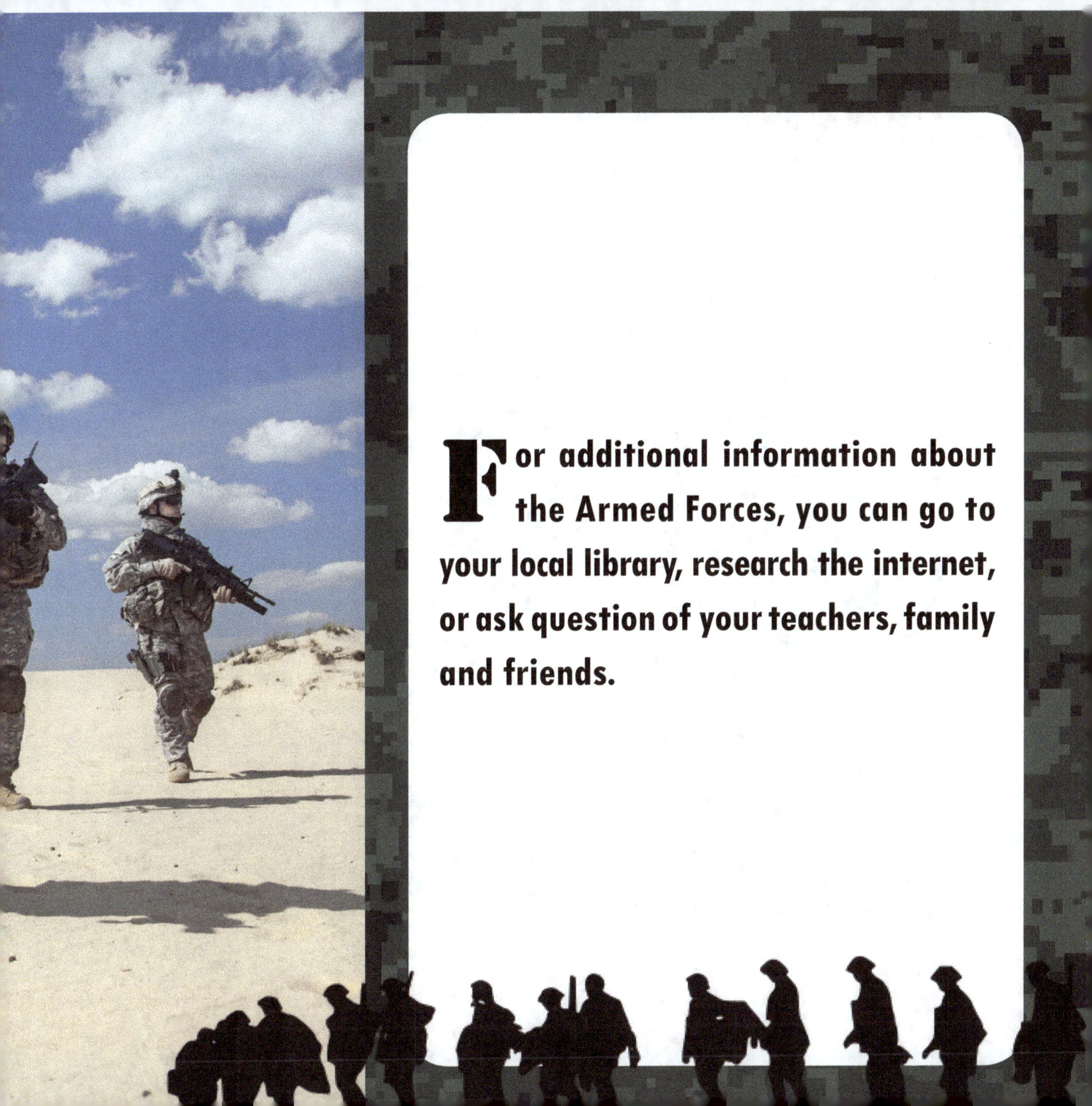

For additional information about the Armed Forces, you can go to your local library, research the internet, or ask question of your teachers, family and friends.

Visit

BABY PROFESSOR
EDUCATION KIDS

www.BabyProfessorBooks.com

to download Free Baby Professor eBooks and view
our catalog of new and exciting Children's Books